Frogs in the Rain Barrel

To Aandy (Shove)
Hope you
enjoy this.

Aaeey Oto
Nov 19 19(

FROGS
IN THE
RAIN BARREL

Sally Ito

NIGHTWOOD EDITIONS

Nightwood Editions
RR.2, S26, C13
Gibsons, BC Canada V0N 1V0

Cover art: Akko Nishimura/Makers' Studio
Cover design: Kim LaFave and Roger Handling
Author photo: Christopher Smith

Canadian Cataloguing in Publication Data

Ito, Sally, 1964–
    Frogs in the rain barrel

    Poems.
    ISBN 0-88971-160-7

    1. Japanese Canadians—Poetry.* I. Title.
PS8567.T6F7 1995   C811'.54   C95-910740-1
PR9199.3.I8F7 1995

Printed in Canada

This book is dedicated to my mother,
Akiko Ito and my father, the late
Kunitaro John Ito.

Contents

Frogs in the Rain Barrel

after collecting, we'd carry them in our hands
    where they became cool pebbles,
still and breathing in the hollow cavern
    of our childish fists.

we'd drop them in the rain barrel
    a small plop,   then,
    the splaying of legs
wriggling in the rippled darkness.

It seemed the rain barrel had no bottom
    just the clear rim of water at its edge,
a pool of still and nether depths
    whose mirrored surface was all.

We thought it an ocean
    for the frogs, we peered over the edge
and watched them swim
    like small shooting stars
bouncing against the rim
    of our reflected faces.

and when they were tired,
    they became still,
their legs and arms outstretched,
        floating,
until their weight collapsed them
    into the palm of our cupped hands.

Sonata for Three Sleeping Women

They are in a room,
together. Their breathing, a rhythm of ages
rises and falls
in the small tempest of sleep.

One is a child, a girl.
Her breath, quick and light
falls as a petal of air
upon a small, rounded face
dreaming of the night's darkness
passing in grace of He
who answers prayers forever.

One is a woman breathing
taut and baited as one who is on the brink
of love's summation; passion
planted in the body,
now growing swollen and wanton
in the night's potted darkness, nurtured
on dreams of a love lasting forever.

And she that is old, sleeps
still, body pulsing to the heart's sound
in the night's boding darkness
where dreams now
lie reverent to the mortal sound
that is not forever. Now
breath for breath's sake.

Begging Bowl

Through the small sorrow
that gathers in my eyes,
      I see my reflection in the shimmering gold
of your flattened figure, bones broken into the bowl
      your mother shaped you into at birth
to replace her cupped hands
      for your hunger and for hers.

You are there in a street full of beggars,
      your shape the only perfect one
amongst the other knobbed and limbless shadows;
      so perfect that even Buddha should be proud
to use you as his alms bowl.

The coins clatter;
your belly contracts
against the dance of metal
on flesh.

And sleeping now in my hotel room,
      the alley closed, I feel your mother's hand
clasp spoon to mouth, rag to face
to wipe away the cool pools of sweat
from my disturbed and restless dreaming.

The Darkness

there is no colour
in darkness,
but the strain of black sound
coming from the fold
above the eye
where God unwittingly dwells.

it is there
in the seeds of fruit—
black stone fixed
in the ripe glitter of colour
in the jungle
where waters slither unseen
into the musk of earth dying.

ah, Kali!
you are neither
goddess nor demon
but the sudden destruction
between limbs
in the Darkness
where Mind is held shut,
by flood released —
where flesh begins
and where it must end.

Maitreya. The Future Buddha

      the finger
is the arc of a crescent moon
        lighting upon the face
of a starless night.

      Such still perfection!
the full tremor of heaven within those lidded eyes,
the smile of seeing on those silent lips.

          poised,
it sits,   an arrow in its bow.

The sudden pull,
      the swift song,
         the toppling body.

     the lotus,
shedding its last petal
   into the clear waters of enlightenment.

Slides of the North

Sachs Harbour, 1959

First,
this one of the snowy owl,
    its leg bound by a string
held by an Inuit boy who grins,
        squatting,
his body a circle of arms and legs
around the thick and feathered white of the owl.

Then here,
beached upon the gravel,
is one of the whale,
    a small, shapely berg,
once the slow, breathing grace of white in water,
now lying collapsed against a sharp and jagged shore.

Now,
the women have gathered about the whale,
their hands a swift rhythm of work,
    curved blades squaring the white
into thick chunks of flesh and blubber;
    a pause for grins,
red smears upon their cheeks and hands.

Next,
is this arctic fox,
a bristling star of fur and snow
    lying crouched to the ground,
chained to the white by
a thick metal clamp,
    traced in a halo of red
upon the dampened snow.

This last shot now,
    a hundred arctic foxes,
frozen carcasses flung one upon the other,
        —the white pyre of legs and heads
posed with the gaping grin of his bounty
    in their open mouths.

Sedna

Once, it is spoken,
there was a woman who birthed
the animals of the sea
from her blood.

They came from her fingers,
shapes swelling from the crimson stripes
left by the hunter's knife. Finned and huge,
they were a painful birth.

She had struggled against him,
pounding against the kayak with her fists,
pounding like a drum,
the first heartbeats of whale and walrus.

He did not hear her cries; silently,
She fell to the ocean's bottom
in the swirl of creatures around her,
their fins grazing her face.

Sedna is the Inuit goddess of the sea. She is said to have been
thrown into the ocean by her desperate father who wanted to
get rid of her because of her mystical powers. She, however,
clung to the boat and only after her father repeatedly slashed her
hands with his knife, did she let go. Out of her blood emerged
the animals of the sea.

The Dead Dolphin

Crozon Peninsula, Brittany

It lay
on a rocky beach
not far from the footpath,

unobtrusive.

The only particular thing
was the stench
and the minute halo of sea gnats
circling around its corpse.

Beyond,
on the cliff,
stone remains
of an ancient
worship site

and a numb and steady
stream of tourists
aching for a blue glimpse
of sea.

Of the Wave

Do you remember
when in my muddled baby English,
I called you,
"Pretty blonde fair eyes princess"
and you smiled, toothless,
without an inkling of a frown
on your five year old face?

We had laughed
high pitched peals,
in our simple nakedness once
when we were six.
Do you remember my touching you there,
when we'd thrown feather pillows
at one another, fast and furious;
hurling, hitting
as if in a blind rage,
until the white down settled onto our skin
where it lay like snow petals
on our childish cracks and curves?

We had splashed
in the bathtub once
when we were seven.
It was after our talk
about the Whelan boys across the street.
We sat prim in the tub
(for Mother had put buns in our hair)
until we began to play.
Do you remember the frenzy
of white froth and bubbles
we created, crouching
like spawning pond frogs.

We grew up
congregated by telephone,
our lipstick a new weapon
heralding the moon
and her cycles of creation.   And yet,
ours was a bold red scrape on white tile and mirror;
graffiti about small socialism in bathrooms
once preserved for 'Jane is a slut' tiles.

Then we sought after knowledge,
you and I.
Our painted nails carved deep crescents
into musty bindings.
Our hands jingled with bracelets and rings
as wrinkled pages were turned, over and over,
by wetted fingertip.
Discourse passed through our reddened lips
in enthused soprano voices.   Cheeks flushed
to each temperament of thought.
The knowledge became
as those pages of our skin
that we sought to caress with our own hands   too often
we could not,
urged by heavy, masculine whispers
hot upon our lobes.

Our precious knowledge did not move
the precious opinion of the others.
Then, you were sad because Descartes was wrong
and I was happy because faith was free.
You left me then, to find perfect answers.
I waited for you. I stopped wondering.
And when you returned, you were older.
And I was with child.

You wondered at the skin of my belly,
bloated and large,
a woman's disfigured testament of love.
And I marvelled still at the sharpness of your mind

We have worshipped different gods,
you and I.   Yet,
time and anatomy still wear
at our bones like the tide upon the sand
that tosses the jewelled shells,
you and I,   sisters,
of the wave.

The Struggle Against Bacchus

We sat, four or perhaps multitudes of us,
in plastic kitchen corners with cafe
lattice outside our window; the patterns
were as fresh as new paint, unstained.

We wore black dresses and blouses,
And assuming George Sand airs, we perfumed
the room heavily with cigar smoke,
wishing that Chopin études were woman-composed.

We sang political slogans in satire
and then, caressing our red bandanna necks,
we let out revolutionary cries of desire
from our once pale lips, now crimson waxed.

We dreamt of sandy beaches and ocean swells
so our looped skirts, white and full,
could become as sails,
Wind-worshipped and beautiful.

Mother

She is strange.
Dwells in the depths of twilight,
wears robes red as the moon drenched in sunset.
Corpses rain down at her feet
like fallen stalks of wheat.

Inside her leafy folds
lies a book of scarlet treasures,
print small and illegible
—tiny dancing spores
from her teeth's
sharp nib.

She is gift giver, oracle.
Seek her at night.
Though she is boding and fierce,
she knits the stars into cloaks
gentle as spring,
and will clothe you,
prepare you
for the coming onslaught of the sun.

Silver Canoe

The moon's silver canoe
glides down night's stream
carrying its heavy load
for the women waiting on the shore.

It comes from far away,
is a piece of a translucent shell,
broken sliver of a sphere
once round and slow moving
in the warm milk
of the universe.

In it all manner of flowers,
sheaves of golden wheat,
stars encased in glass baubles,
strung on thin threads
made of spider's webs.

When they see it,
they dance on the shore,
thin, pale faced mothers,
hunched widows, young girls
in white.

The grass is fresh with tears,
dew bitten strands of green
bind their feet,
curl around their ankles,
as they move closer to the shore

Why Did You Tell Me Lies About Foreign Countries?

When you slept in the savanna
with a lioness's pelt as your bed,
the negress whom you paid to sleep with
must have smiled her rotten teeth
as she sang of your glassy tears
upon her pockmarked belly.

On a beach of star strewn pebbles,
you lay orange in a Polynesian sunset
with Gauguin models by your side, —
barely clothed, skin shiny as satin,
bones exposed like contours
of scenery on a coloured canvas.

Somewhere in Japan, amidst the cars and companies,
a large, clouded temple of lacquered wood
must glow eminently like a Sony Video commercial
in Times Square. Your kimonoed ladies, like mist,
must forever dance in pine boughs
where no one can see them.

And still, you speak of your heaven and hell
with angels and demons so incandescent and glowing
as to burn out your eyes with their intensity. And yet,
addressing the ceiling, I feel only the muscles
in your belly contract above mine,
in abated ecstasy.

I feel your phallus gyrating in my womb,
exploding its load of stories into me.
Am I another story, a womb to forge your exotic fantasy?

Truth, I suppose, escapes you, like your seed
into a woman who shall later bleed,
even with your memory.

Salmon Run

Sometimes in the night,
        I find you spawning in my bed
as if the sheets were the last, wrinkling folds
    of the stream that is to claim your life.

The incessant thumping of your tail
    against my back is filled with the frenzy of mating;
your spine curves and wiggles, the scales glisten
    with the plashing of sweat,
the bed is shallow and muddied.

Sometimes, I dream I am a large bear
    pawing at the fading, silver crescent
as if I were the starry Ursa
    feeding upon the spent flesh of the moon.

Night in Prospector's Valley
Kootenay National Park

we bed early,
the fall of night
heavy as water
on the stone walls
around us.

so dark is it,
we cannot see
the circle of the mountains,
the curve of the glacier,
the pools of water in the meadow,
that flushed before our eyes
at dawn.

it is like a bear,
this darkness—
as if we had bedded in its very fur,
nestling in what we fear most
of this wilderness.

such is the darkness of the mind
before awakening—a shadow, dense and thick,
lumbering upon the grassy slope,
til the snowy edge catch its foot,
and breaks its shape
—a spilled handful of stars
that light the night sky.

Jews in Old China

I

Their history
is without words
in this ancient land.

Who carries the struggle
but the oak, the voices
in the still branches?

II

The silk road
winds around their middles
like sashes of birds in flight
over the soundless plain.

A ringing bell,
and they are sudden scattered
pearls in a
wave of blue silk.

III

These sages
cut across pages
of black ink
and rice paper.

Searching, searching.

The fine stroke of the brush,
the black flutter of words,
the sudden rush of wind

and their story is revealed.

Chinese Oldtimer

Via Rail Terminal, Vancouver, B.C.

He sat solitary
amidst a circle of boxes,
bound and rebound in twined string,
sides scribbled with faded Chinese characters
promising canned oranges, lotus root
and pickled ginger.

A circle of clucking relatives
moved around him
'Time for Grandfather to move.'
—move to the next grudging
son in Calgary.

The train whistled its last call.

He got on,
a pocket full of change, a stick of gum,
and a piece of an old
porcelain dragon that he had broken
while packing.

Outside, Vancouver began moving away
a city of light strewn upon the water—
a sight the old man had seen long ago
from the porthole of a freighter.
His brown skinned eyes, then filled with
the wondering glow of the new and curious
had now grown wrinkled and half closed,
pupils passing light through an
obscure halo of white.

The rails began to click and click
the passing song of the Golden Mountain,
a dream that was only a clear
mountain stream flowing pure and transient
down a steep hill of crushed gravel
used to build the CPR.

Winter's Bride

(Monologue of an Immigrant Wife)

I cannot hate this country
though the way frost clings to trees here
cleaves me to you in whitened crystal,
immobile and beautiful.
And if I should chide you
for bringing me here,
it would be like addressing a tall pine,
forever green, thriving
as only a plant indigenous could
in a land as cold and frigid as this.
Forgive me if I am cold,
I, the whitest snowflake,
cannot melt in this country
—cannot melt into your arms;
When perhaps at home
I could've fluttered
in a blue sky dance;
white star, melting
into the dark, rich earth
so that you might have spoken the soft praise
of my passing resilience to you.
Instead, you wish to freeze and preserve me
in an icicle showcase of glass.
My tears need only drip further
for you to see me grow
in sorrow magnified by the cold
you have inflicted upon me.
No, but I cannot hate this country
for you have brought me here to stay.
A spectacle of culture, frozen,
I shall remain,
in cold pride, cold disdain.

Portrait of Snow Country

Brown house-shacks cluster together as
flakes float and settle upon their wooden roofs;
silence in this valley slowly creeps in and moves.
Winter has finally arrived. Snow cold weather.
Black trains pull in, bleating faraway calls,
their billowed smoke fading into the white air
as more passengers arrive to this 'somewhere'
interior built of nature's shale and limestone walls.
A mountain sketch reveals white sentinel peaks
looming over an old man and his young son,
squatting on their porch, looking into the darkened horizon;
faces flat and dull, colour faded from their cheeks.
A photograph taken, words later scribbled in the corner,
'Father and I on the porch, Winter of '42, New Denver.'

Sansei

i am at my Teacher's house
for my first calligraphy lesson.
Grandmother has given me her old brush
                              and her old inkstone
                              and a blessing
from her faraway Japan lips.

i see the cat
in Teacher's study
for the first time.   it is very white and
                              of a pure strain
                of breed
i cannot quite recognize   yet.

it looks at me,   queerly.
i notice a fringe of black
around its paws. upon the desk
is a clutter of rice paper
splattered thick in black
with the inked tracks
of a strolling cat.

'that which prints
its true nature
is what is real.'
Teacher once said.

if that is so, then i know
                the spirit of a Sansei
                              sleeps, still dormant
                              in the pit of that white belly.

Sansei is a third generation Japanese Canadian

Roots

In the fogged and dreary places
of the still immediate past,
my descendants walked the docks
in brown shaded clothing
in yellowed photographs.
Smiles were uncommon then
(a sort of immorality, maybe).
See here, in this old photo—
Grandfather, the fisherman,
grey net delicately fondled in his palm;
Mother with the black bowl cut, stains on her frock,
fingers in her mouth—Uncle with his schoolboy shorts on,
hunched forward, hands on his thighs.
Behind them, is the boat;
its fuzzily shaped prow bears only the name
"Suzuki"—a 'common as horseshit on the road' name
Grandfather would say
though he'd never change the bold lettering on the prow
for his life.
The boat, since confiscated,
is now long gone, disappeared
like my Grandfather whose wrinkled flesh, satiny
to the touch, has left the kitchen chair
for a rich-earth plot. The flowers on this place
do nothing to the grey headstone
I, the living one, see each spring.
My mind, accustomed to education,
the ways of schooled truth and justice,
is still attracted to the black etched
"Suzuki"—a 'common as horseshit on the road' name.
No more horseshit on the road anymore, Grandfather.
Just a multitude of cars and bikes bearing the name
of my confiscated identity.

On Translating the Works of Akiko Yosano

To the Akiko who is my mother.

It is hard to believe
she is you.

Her hair, wisps of dreams,
spread tangled
on the chest of her poet-lover
is now your sleeping head,
a prayer of darkness,
just before morning.

I rouse you from your sleep
with a long distance call, asking,
"What is 'sasashigeri'? What does it mean?"

And you answer,

"Don't you remember Nanzen Temple
—the way the grass grows there,
lush and thick, like the way your hair
used to trail through my hands,
rustling in impatience with my comb?"

It was as if I had woken you
from your dreaming, my harsh questions
clattering like bamboo sticks
upon the smooth stones of your memory.

You say,

"Translating poetry is impractical."

as if it were impractical
to rouse from your memory, this longing
for my childhood,
and the image of a temple
twenty years past.

'sasashigeri' means thick bamboo grass.

Riding to the Capital

Riding on the train
to the capital,
    I see, sitting across from me,
a schoolboy.

And through the rattling windows,
a running stream of gray buildings and factories—
thick, smoke-coloured fins fanning
at our eyes.

Immaculately dressed,
    attended to by his young mother
fussing over the collar white of his neck,
over his plump knee-socked legs,

they are riding to the capital.

    A hiss of track,
A flash of silver,
        and sudden quavering dome
the din of human effort,
    a cluster of weeds
        rooted in sand.

    And the schoolboy
with his mother,
        puts on his jacket, shoulders his bag,
clutches his mother's hand
    as if direction
were but to a capital of singing tracks,
still racing with our labouring hands.

Kyoto

Book of knowledge said:
  a city of cultural splendour
  housing the nation's most
  historically revered pieces of art.

Voice of Grandmother says:
  ah, city of palaces and castles
  built up in gold and silver
  for emperors and lords clothed
  in kimonos of the purest silk.

Kyoto in my head:
     a city of light nestled in mtns
        mtns to climb
     mtns to worship
     mtns to crumble, fall away   for me
                    to see
    what has been there
       for ages.

Kyoto II

      diary of a visit

kyoto station
early spring

             you meet me here,
    an appointed guide, my relative,
      (we look astonishingly alike).
         Knowing
  too well what i seek, you say at once,
     'Kyoto is a city of ephemeral delight.

To hold the most fleeting sight within
the palm of your eye is to catch
the heart of your imagined place.'

✿

late night
downtown kyoto

tonight, i caught glimpse of her
of whom you spoke, flitting into the night;
a sleeve, red as blood, flashing from
a geisha hurrying into a limousine
down a Gion alleyway.

even here and now,
        you say the sight is rare.
        Rare as what?
        Me in my kimono
                        Or you in yours?

✿

hot springs
mtns near kyoto

                        naked
in the spring, i bathe
quietly in the corner—
my body exposed, pale and white
        against the colored tile.
                you offer to scrub my back.

i nod.
        Hearing
only the quiet chuffing of your
hands upon my skin, i think
        'how loud
        the sound of insects
        humming in the night.'

                    ✳

last day,
omuro, kyoto

                        And oh,
        the cherry trees are in bloom!
        We have gone to Omuro Temple to see
                the late blossoms
                    worshipped for centuries by courtiers
                and priests,
                    and merchants
                and yes, even you
        who claims veteran this world of transience—
                you, who saved for me, two pink petals,
                soft as a child's cheek, to put in my pocket
                for me to find at the train station.

                'ah, train fare
                        fare for home.'—Parting gift
                        too fragile for the
                        station clerk's punch.

Winter Plum

It stands forlorn,
       this winter plum,
an abandoned nest
   between its branches.

But on each crook,
      the frail flush of pink;
sparks of defiance
   in this dreary November.

Like a young woman
   about to run away,
the blossoms shudder and quake
   in the wind,
the branches rustle
   in haste for spring.

Only the bird's nest
      remains still and ruinous.
Already,   a feather fallen
to the snow touched ground.

Crocus

The emergence
      of its self
is a reminder of renewal.

               There are
many more flowers,
          blossoms,
to shed their gowns
in this season's dawn.

       But the crocus
is first. Its eyes open,
        it is the first to see,
   to witness the carnage of winter.
It will lay on winter's grave
its bowl shaped, penitent petals,
so it may ask
the straying eye to pause
upon its poverty, to fill its bowl
with the wonder of spring.

The Mountain of Broken Glass

On the mountain of broken glass,
there are many shards of mirrors,
bottles, glasses, windows.

Everything you can see through
is piled here in small sharp bits.

Everywhere you step,
there is danger.

All mountains are made of glass:
blue frosted triangles
orange tinted pyramids
mirrored green crystals.

They are what pushed out of the ground
from the sea,   blue and tranquil sheets
of water,   hardened, shattered, broken
sea of dreams that we climb
once again,
carefully, so carefully,
so not to cut or scratch
our frail, fractured reflections.

Prayer Wheel, Tibet

Its persistent squeaking
can be heard through the valley
as hands hurl to heaven
   prayers, desires,
the simple wants of earth.

Children run indifferently in the snow.

On each wheel,
   the picture of civilization,
a prayer of gold, the lustre of suffering
painstakingly etched, now smudged and worn.

Upon these cold, nameless gods
our steaming breath, the stench of life.

The wheel is turned,
   and into the wind-tossed sky
prayers are borne—
   a flood of penitent stars
filling the dark, blue void.

Pangaea

Wegener had it right.
We are all from the same continent,
from the same void
of disturbed memories.

Our feet, swift and light,
traversed the plain
through night's darkness;
set up tents near water,
breathed air pure as sound.

No gulf or expanse of water
threatened our vision;
no animal skirted our sight
into the unknown.
Everything was knowledge,
accessible
and defined as sunlight
on our hands.

More than hundreds or millions of years
will have passed,
and all kindred will claim that earth
never split, that it was always whole,
that there was never rift nor river
to break the earth's surface.

But the earth knows its painful birth,
remembers its limbs torn and cracked,
how animals frantic and desperate
stampeded across its yawning chasms
and folding mountains, and we
who have forgotten,
will stumble across
it in our dreams

as Wegener did,
and wonder at the startling
similarity of our thoughts
as they traverse plains,
come to edges,
and fall softly,   soundlessly,
into the ocean's gleaming waters.

Wegener is the scientist who developed the theory of
continental drift. Pangaea was the name he gave to the original
land mass that existed before it split apart to form the various
continents.

Garment

Watch the way Inuit women
sew with their teeth,
soften the hides
with their saliva,
chew at the sinewy edges

A hide is a landscape
harsh, brittle as ice,
a cold, glittering skin
of snow

Labor over it,
warm it with your breath

and it will form a skin
around your body
as it once did caribou
    fox,
     seal,

embrace you, hunter,
brute.

The Vehicle

In a distant temple
in a bustling city,
Master asks Novice,
"Does the Dog have Buddha-nature?"

"MU!" roars the Novice

who sudden bounds ahead a field
   of yelping hounds, pulling at their leashes
whining after the elusive fox

    whose cunning wit, the charm
of a red-haired woman in a Shakespeare play,
    has suddenly disappeared, lost its scent
in a nearby stream,   dimpling, babbling
    the songs of glory;

    a crop of daffodils bursts upon the bank,
and the fox is no more,
    but the scent of its being
drifts by winds to a northern shore,

    rugged, cold
where now the echoed Novice's reply
    repeats against each stony wall,
each towering pine, grows around itself
    a silver coat of fur,   and prowls by night
in dreams,   sudden, vast, white.

Sea Turtle

By night,
they come onto shore,
their awkward fins
flapping against the sand
to where they will
bury their eggs.

Whole maps of the sea's belly
are carved on their shells;
faint valleys and ridges,
filled with the sigh of whales,
the song of porpoises,
the dance of seaweed.

Urashima Taro,
the fisherman who rode
the sea turtle's back
will tell you a story

of how time,
once stopped,
is never retrieved,

is only a silver thread of smoke
from a small black box
fetched from the sea
by a sea turtle's slow, wide paddle
down, down   into the teeming landscape
beyond our eye's dim edge.

The story of Urashima Taro is the Japanese version of the Rip
Van Winkle myth. Urashima Taro was a fisherman who rode
down to the Palace of the Sea on a sea turtle's back. The King
of the Sea gave him a special box as a gift. When he returned to
his village, he no longer recognized anyone. He opened the box
and a silver wisp of smoke turned him into an old man.

Poetry

Waves that sigh
are best recorded in dreams
where their meaning is
not obscure.

Still we continue
chiselling words in sand,
have them washed away by Leviathan,
only to begin again.

But comes the day we drop the chisel
and grope after the silvery tail
disappearing into the sea

and oh, what of the scales left in our hands!
opalescent bits of glass
through which our Self may be mirrored,
darkly, darkly,
as the night from which
this monster came.

Zero

When I was a child
zero was a difficult concept
for me.

The man who tried to teach me
with infinite patience
would hold up his hand
with five fingers,
now four,
three,
two,
one,
and then a fist,
and I was suddenly baffled.

There was no steeple
        for air to swirl around,
no pole for winds
to chase ribbons about,
no stick in the sand
for waves to swell and surround,

For around that fist
was perfect stillness.
The puzzled 'oh' that came from
my mouth, would circle,
predatory and wondering
around that closed hand
waiting for some
childish illumination
to suddenly spring out
from between the fingers.

It was not until much later
that I was to find
that zero was the last
of numbers to be discovered.
It seemed to have never existed,
never have been,
until with perfect excitement
someone traced a line
to enclose that space,
that sudden gap of time
we had not yet seen or felt.

Jeremiah

Prophecy is a circle,
        a halo of syllables,
burning my mouth, a curse
that suddenly pulls me
down into this hole,
a cave in the rock.

What caused these words, ungainly and hideous
            to crawl from my mouth,
suddenly lion-legged and swift,
as creeping night onto a grazing animal,
I cannot say,   only that I sit in solitude,
so that I may devour each word and sound
ripped from the bone.

In the painful darkness
of this hole,   around me on the wall,
are clinging clods of dirt — huge dissembled portions
gather about my head like a hillside crowd
awaiting my sudden blow of breath,
my scatter of spittle on their brows,
and like the jug about to be shattered,
my arm rises threateningly only
to dislodge the ceiling
onto my head.

My words are brass,
polished and gleaming, and with this,
they have built a wall,
an impenetrable reflection of myself.

It is this reflection
that blinds me, that burns holes in my eyes,
In the darkness, my feet stumbled
over hills, tripped into night
like a fallen animal.

I do not fear captivity.
I am already captured.   Inside this hole
are many birds that sit upon my hands and knees,
girting my body with Your belt
like leaves to an almond tree,
ready soon,
to burst forth
out of this desert wilderness.

On Meeting the Prophet: Five Stages

Seeking the Prophet's thumb
    like seeds among stones,
are hands, blooming frail
    the flowers of His sowing.

Savouring the Prophet's cries
    like fruit, all bruised
are golden scattered,   a flock of sheep,
    a swarm of flies.

Wearing the Prophet's face
    like gems upon water,
are two eyes,   clever frogs!
    green stones of silence.

Shedding the Prophet's gown
    like wind undressing,
are restless scents, quaking lilac
    shuddering rose.

Riding the Prophet's tail
    like water rolling off the dewy leaf,
the still sounds of His flight
    are bells, clear as the new moon.

The Seven Stones of Paradise

There are seven stones
each in your hand.

They are gardens.
          Slow and circular
like suns, your hands
grow around them.

And seeds like spring
          force through
the crevice of your fingers,
          a flower'd burst of crimson.

Like prophets
          unveiling seven truths,
your hands let go,
          the seven birds of heaven.

Hannah's Prayer

Eli thought she was a drunken woman,
her lips, a silent orgy
of mutterings and groans.

"Nay, but it is not so,"
she cried,
I am praying, my lord,
in anguish and despair"

For I am barren.
Though in love's garden,
my portion is double
this is not enough.

Around me grow the young stalks
of another that taunt and whisper,
each golden head a laughing rebuttal
against my womb.

The leaves that should shade
are dense and malicious clusters
of darkness that blot and mar
my longing eye's heavenward glance.

How can I but weep
on this fertile ground
where green is everywhere present,
everywhere burning on my brow, my hands,
the soles of my feet?

Oh my Lord,
grant me but one child,
and it is yours!

from out of this garden
will I bring it forth,
lay it on your temple gates,
offer it to you,
your child,
your gift.

Remember me, my Lord.
Remember your servant, Hannah.

Dreaming of Jerusalem

Sometimes in the night
I am seized by absolute darkness.
Black, bristling thorns
stumble across my forehead
in a blind march towards death.

❁

Six miles of Jerusalem
stretch out before me in my sleep.
Everywhere sand,
and the distant jockeying of stars
heralding the great birth
of a new   what?

Along that ancient sea,
    footsteps
soft as the moon's breath on the water
grace the shore,   stop at the pebbled fragment
of land,

and a glimpse of that glittering city
skips across the eye,
burns like live coals,
sears in the palm
crimson buds,   two bright windows
from which to see Paradise.

A Priest's Advice

'When you build a city,
the first thing you must build
is the church,'
the priest told me.

'The church should be made
primarily of stone,
big stones, preferably grey,
quarried in large chunks
and brought to what will be
the centre of the city.

Do you understand?'
he asks me.

'These days,
cities do not care
about their churches;
they are concerned with
other kinds of growth,
mostly economic, and so
churches have been sadly neglected.

But you must not be like this yourself'
he instructs,
'Do not litter the square
with these large stones abandoned
for some other great project.
Stones have no meaning if left like that,
untended pieces of mountain,
cold, grey bits of hardened clouds.
Stones are foundations.
Breathe into them
and they will roll away,
reveal to you secrets
hitherto unknown.'

Rachel

I have not met a man
so strong as the snake
who grabbed my ankles
and wrestled me to the ground.

No, not even you, Jacob.

If in that night,
I had a branch,
I would have chased it off.

But the enormity of it,
the promise of its poison!

At long last,
the liberating of my thighs
to the cry of birth.

Forgive me, dear Jacob, forgive me

but I too have wrestled,
wrestled like you,
with this monster
called Love.

Ruth

Ruth the Moabite
is all that we should be
when we love.

When we glean the fields
for the litter of stars
and their fallen heads of gold,
we reap not what was left
but what is truly ours.

No man owns the fields,
a claim to something ephemeral
as growth and decay.

Ruth is love,
is the laying down of our bodies
in their finest raiment
for the sleeping kinsman,
Redeemer.

Joseph

i wore the coat of many colors,
was favored

and i had dreams,
oh such dreams,
that were a pleasure
to my rainbow colored self —

how the sheaves
in their many skirts of gold
bowed their crowned heads
to me,

how the sun and the moon
with their white haired flock of stars
circled round me in obeisance.

i was the planet
around which all revolved,
ego's bright gem of colors.

and so, I told my brothers,
became the kernel of their contempt.

They threw me in a pit,
took away my precious coat,
shred it, bathed it in blood
and lied to my father.

Naked, thirsty, alone
did i stand in that pit,
in that circling fist
of earth and clay.

And then did i see
in one night's eye
the trimming of His coat,
that magic cloak of colors
around which all earth is wrapped,
how i glimpsed the domed edge,
a fringe of stars and planets
fluttering in that vast
wonder of blue silk

and how i saw in it,
humbly,

my reflection,
bloodied, tattered.

Mendeleev

He charted the unseen
                whirling particles of energy,
rotating like suns around the soul.

         How in his ponderous hands,
they became as tangible as fireflies caught
in an open field,   how with meticulous grace,
he was able to bottle them,
          puncture the lids with a precise
number of holes.

This particular penchant for order,
         this fine and disturbed desire for precision
measures the breathing of souls
in the deepest sleep,   measures too,
the sound of crickets in the early darkness,
          the ebb of water on the shore.

Birds that suddenly scatter
will form lines
to alert us to this order, this almost palpable
hand of heaven guiding our eyes
to conclusions,
thoughts,
memories,
and prayers.

In the midst of our counting,
                we are able to see stars dance
and shape our histories,   see heroes battle in storms
         of lightning and sand, see flowers bloom and wilt
in youth's simple light.

Mendeleev,
　　　　your dreams of ordering
this swirling universe, this dense cluster of activity
is a limitless task,　　beguiling as they are,　these
soft luminescent bodies that flicker into the night,
　　　　trailing behind them
the gossamer threads of energy.

Dmitri Mendeleev created the Periodic Table used in chemistry.

Calvaire

As if the church
were not enough,
they stand a few hundred metres away,
grey stone stories of saints
martyred, murdered,
slain, and slaughtered

and there are
veiled and weeping women,
perfect tears
of stone trickling
down their cheeks.

And always on top
of the circling round,
the man on the stone cross
perched,
his worn and weary head
crowned with the sky's
uncertain blue.

Calvaires are cross-shaped stone monuments depicting various
biblical and Christian myths, built by churches in Brittany.

Kumba

For Jeremie

The Soul is in the Kumba
he says,
    dancing like a fish,
fins moving through the air,   "See now
how He eats,   that big Spirit in the sky
        when you die.
He eats your soul, whole,
        brother
like the whale who ate
my brother, Jonah.

        Push dem hips forward
he says   Push dem fast

like a gun,   you gotta shoot Him
like a sister,   you gotta praise Him
        you gotta love Him
        you gotta kill Him

And the ladies cry,
hips to the sky,
where they are singing,
       swinging
to the rhythm of the seas.

Everyone's born in sufferin'
he says
Everyone grows in sufferin'
he says,
and Everyone dies in sufferin'

and he says
there's no answer but for dancin'
not dancin' like the white man
not dancin' like the black man

but dancin' like the Soul man
and I say now,   swim, brother, swim
Swim like you've swum no race before.

And I tell you now,   he says
     Dis Love is too high for me
     Dis Love is too deep for me
     Dis Love,   Dis Love
     is not a hundred plus a hundred
     not a thousand plus a thousand
     but a million times a million
     too big for me, dis love for you and me.

and he swims, he swims
like a fish,   fins moving through the air,
head full of hymns, dancing hands of prayer.

Kumba means 'belly.'

The Green Fire

There is a green fire
in the grass,

a green fire
whose flames lick
at the blue
centre of my heart
where the thousand tiny
seeds of Demeter lie.

Love has set its fire
in the midst of a granary;
let loose its snaking flames
over the cool waves of yellow.

To the very belly of those seeds
are those fingerlings reaching,
licking,   lapping,   darting
            iridescent
tongues of green pushing, pushing.

Every seed is an eye of Isis,
every seed the eye of breath
from which vapours string the air,
bind the blue winds
into pillars of white.

o love
that i may hold that snake!
let it coil round me
            my neck and shoulders,
my waist,   my thigh!

Let it return   at last
to the earthen pot from which
the charmer
raised its singing shape

o snake of eden!

In my mother's jewellery box
is a ring, blue green opal
nestled in a velvet slit of red

and there is a story a long time ago
of a sailor from Mexico
and a young Japanese woman in Yokohama
and how the glistening sea came
between them, swirled around
their clasped hands,
hardened into stone.

What is the green fire?

It is a flame
that enters
the sanctuary,

that sets fire
to the garden.

o in the mtns
was it there!
that we wrmed our hands
ovr its breath
rolled in splndr
in its blnkts of green
and how the snow
envied us   hrled its
angry charm of slt
ovr our naked sleeping bdies
where the flames
hid in shallow pool of our flesh,
grew in the hollow
of our bellies

it is only
a reflection,

a winding path of
blue smoke from this
green hearth

up the trunk
of the aged tree
from which Love hung,
His fiery crown of doves
left in our trembling hands.

I wish to acknowledge the encouragement and support of my creative writing teachers—George McWhirter of UBC and Bert Almon of the University of Alberta—in the preparation of this manuscript. I also would like to thank my family and especially my husband, Paul Dyck, for their patience and love.